6/01

D0130801

Palo Alto City Library

The individual borrower is responsible for all library
material borrowed on his or her card.

Charges as determined by the CITY OF PALO
ALTO will be assessed for each overdue item.

Damaged or non-returned property will be billed to
the individual borrower by the CITY OF PALO ALTO.

P.O. Box 10250, Palo Alto, CA 94303

LETTERS HOME
from the
GRAND CANYON

Lisa Halvorsen

BLACKBIRCH PRESS, INC.
WOODBRIDGE, CONNECTICUT

Published by Blackbirch Press, Inc.
260 Amity Road
Woodbridge, CT 06525

©2000 by Blackbirch Press, Inc.
First Edition

e-mail: staff@blackbirch.com
Web site: www.blackbirch.com

Printed in Singapore

10 9 8 7 6 5 4 3 2 1

All photographs ©Corel Corporation

Library of Congress Cataloging-in-Publication Data
Halvorsen, Lisa.
Grand Canyon / by Lisa Halvorsen.
    p.   cm. — (Letters home from national parks)
Includes bibliographical references and index.
Summary: This first-person account of a trip to the Grand Canyon describes some of its out-
standing features including unusual plants and animals, strange formations, waterfalls, and trails.
ISBN 1-56711-463-6
1. Grand Canyon National Park (Ariz.)—Juvenile literature. 2. Grand Canyon (Ariz.)—
Juvenile literature. [1. Grand Canyon National Park (Ariz.) 2. Grand Canyon (Ariz.) 3.
National parks and reserves] I. Title. II. Series.
F788 .H23 2000   99-050075
979.1'32—dc21   CIP
                                                                                  AC

TABLE OF CONTENTS

Arrival in. . .

Las Vegas

I can't believe I'm standing on the edge of the Grand Canyon. It's enormous! Everywhere I look, I see bands of red, orange, yellow, and even purple rock. There are so many interesting rock shapes and formations. And lots of people! More than 5 million people from all over the world visit the canyon each year.

The Grand Canyon is located in northwestern Arizona, near the border of Utah and Nevada. It is 1 mile deep and up to 18 miles wide. Altogether, it is 277 miles long. It is not the deepest canyon in the world, but it's probably the most famous. Some people call it America's national treasure. It is also considered one of the seven natural wonders of the modern world.

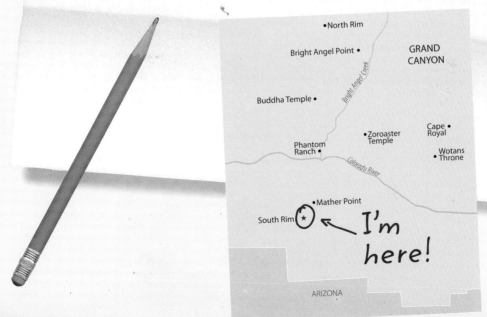

North Rim

Bright Angel Point •

GRAND CANYON

Bright Angel Creek

Buddha Temple •

• Zoroaster Temple

Cape • Royal

Phantom Ranch

Colorado River

Wotans • Throne

• Mather Point

South Rim ⊙← I'm here!

ARIZONA

Grand Canyon

I read a book about the canyon during our plane flight. It said the canyon formed about 6 million years ago. The mighty Colorado River carved it out of the Colorado Plateau. The canyon walls tell a story that goes back 2 billion years. Each layer, or stratum, is a different rock type that formed at a different time. Many contain fossils of insects, sea animals, and creatures that lived before the age of dinosaurs!

The top band of limestone makes up the youngest layer. It's 240 million years old. If you think of the canyon as a big bathtub, this layer is the ring at the top of the tub. The bottom layer of dark gray rock, called vishnu schist, is 1.7 billion years old. That's about one-third the age of Earth!

Rainbow over Grand Canyon

Grand Canyon

Butte shaped by erosion

My book said archaeologists have found signs that ancient Indians lived in the area as long as 4,000 years ago. The first outsider, Captain García López de Cárdenas of New Spain (now Mexico), "found" the canyon in 1540. He was originally looking for the Seven Cities of Gold. While searching, he'd heard an incredible story about a huge hole in the ground. After weeks of looking, he finally found it. Unfortunately, he couldn't find a way to climb down the steep canyon walls.

South Rim Entrance

When we arrived yesterday, we stopped at the visitor center on the South Rim to find out more about Grand Canyon National Park. We were surprised to learn that 90% of the park's visitors view the canyon only from the South Rim. They never take one of the corridor trails to the bottom of the canyon or travel to the North Rim.

The park covers 1,955 square miles. That's about the size of Delaware! In addition to unusual natural formations, more than 3,500 archeological sites have been uncovered. There are also many 19th-century mining camps.

South Rim of Grand Canyon

Guide explaining the canyon

Morning light on South Rim

The ranger told us that if we walked from the canyon floor to the North Rim, it would be like going from the Mexican desert to southern Canada. That's how much the climate and the vegetation differ.

I was excited to learn that more than 88 species of mammals, 58 species of reptiles and amphibians, 26 species of fish, and 287 different species of birds live in the park. Some are found nowhere else in the world, like the Kaibab squirrel and the Grand Canyon rattlesnake.

President Benjamin Harrison was the first to protect the park. In 1893, he made it a forest reserve. In 1908, President Theodore Roosevelt designated the area a national monument. Then in 1919, President Woodrow Wilson signed a bill to make the Grand Canyon a national park.

9

Mather Point

Like most visitors, we got our first look at the canyon from Mather Point. From this lookout I could see all the way to the North Rim on the other side of the canyon! Although it's only 10 miles away, it takes most hikers at least 2 days to hike from rim to rim. That's because they have to hike down a steep trail, cross the Colorado River, and then walk back up the other side.

Morning sun on Mather Point

Mather Point

Sunrise over
Vishnu Temple

From Mather Point, we followed East Rim Drive to Desert View. We saw many strange rock formations with names like Wotans Throne, Zoraster Temple, and Brahma Temple. My favorite was Duck-on-a-Rock. The "temples" were named by Clarence Dutton. In 1881, he did the first geological survey of the canyon. The rocks, with their high spires, reminded him of temples in China and India.

At the Desert View Overlook, I climbed the 65-foot-high Watchtower. Wow! Now I know what a raven feels like when it's flying high above the canyon!

Down the South Wall

After spending a day on the rim, I'm excited about going down into the inner canyon. You have to walk or ride a mule. The ranger advised us to carry lots of water, and to make sure we returned by dusk. (You need a permit for overnight trips.) He also warned us to watch where we step. That's because scorpions and rattlesnakes hide under rocks. Their bites are very painful and can be dangerous—sometimes even deadly.

Two main trails zigzag, or switchback, down the canyon walls from the South Rim. We chose the Bright Angel Trail. It leads to the Colorado River and then the River Trail. It is not as steep as the South Kaibab Trail.

Trail down the canyon wall

Switchback on canyon trail

Mule riders

This is a hiker's paradise! There are 400 miles of trails in the park! Many of them were made by prospectors. They came here in the late 1800s in search of copper, zinc, and lead. Some found they could make more money by taking visitors to see the canyon. Other trails were formed by deer, big-horn sheep, and early Native Americans.

The bottom of the canyon is a desert. In summer, it can get as hot as 120 degrees Farenheit. That's 35 degrees hotter than at the rim. In winter, when there's 12 feet of snow up on the rim, flowers are still in bloom in the canyon!

Colorado River

The Colorado River is one of the most famous landmarks in the park. It's 1,450 miles long. About 277 miles flow through the Grand Canyon. It is the longest river west of the Rocky Mountains. It begins in northern Colorado just west of the Continental Divide. The river winds through seven states and Mexico before it reaches the Gulf of California.

The Spanish called the river Rio Colorado or "Red River." That's because sediment used to give it a muddy, red color. But in 1963, the Glen Canyon Dam was erected to prevent sediment from building up behind the Hoover Dam on the other end of the canyon. Now the water is blue-green.

Grand Canyon painted with light

The Great Chasm

Colorado reflections

Small beach on Colorado River

In the early 1900s, Emery and Ellsworth Kolb traveled down the winding river to make a film. The film showed people what it was like to "run the rapids." This movie has been shown in the park for 60 years. That makes it the longest continuously running motion picture in history!

Today the National Park Service limits the number of people on the river. This helps prevent erosion and damage to the environment.

River Rafting

Today we learned that Major John Wesley Powell was the first person to travel the entire length of the Colorado River. His trip took him through an unexplored section of water that ran through the Grand Canyon. He had no map, and faced many unknown dangers, like fast-moving rapids.

But what's really amazing is that he did this with only one arm! He'd lost his right arm at the Battle of Shiloh in the Civil War. After the war, he became a professor of geology in Illinois. Then, in 1869, he set out to explore the Colorado River. He and his nine men paddled down the river in four small wooden boats. Sadly, not everyone survived the trip.

Colorado River

Rafting in the Grand Canyon

Deer Creek Falls

Today, if you want to see the canyon by water, you can sign up for a river rafting trip. All start at Lees Ferry. The trips take you through stretches of fast-moving white water, and past sandy beaches and high rock walls. Sometimes, if the water is too rough, you have to get out and walk. At night you camp along the river. Occasionally there is time to explore the side canyons or ancient Pueblo Indian sites.

There are more than 150 rapids in the park. Lava Falls are the largest and roughest rapids on the river. They drop 37 feet, like a mini-waterfall. The average depth of the river is 20 feet. The water is very cold and has a strong current. It is not a safe place to swim.

Ancient Pueblo

The ancient Pueblo are ancestors of today's Hopi and Zuni Indians. These ancient Indians have also been called Anasazi, which is a Navajo word meaning "ancient ones." These Native Americans lived in the canyon between 500 to 1,500 years ago. They lived in pueblos, or villages, in or near cliffs.

These early people made baskets from the yucca plant to carry water, food, and tools. Later, they made pottery out of the red clay of the canyon. They also built channels and small dams to capture rainwater. This water was used for drinking, and to water their crops of maize (corn), beans, and squash. More than 2,000 ancient Pueblo ruins have been found in the park. We visited the Tusayan Ruin near the east entrance to the park. It is 800 years old.

Baked mud in the river bottom

Pueblo ruins

Ancient Indians

Archaeologists have found proof of an even earlier civilization, from about 4,000 years ago. It's called the Desert Culture. These forefathers of the ancient Pueblo are believed to have been mainly hunters and gatherers. Most may have lived in pit houses near the canyon, but not in the canyon itself.

After the ancient Pueblo disappeared, other tribes like the Cerbat, Navajo, and Paiute arrived. The Paiute called the area Kaibab, which means "mountain lying down."

Flowers bursting from rock

Tower based on Ancient Pueblo

Havasu Canyon/Falls

Today the Havasupai, descendants of the Cerbats, live in Havasu Canyon. It is a side canyon on the western end of the Grand Canyon. This tribe of 650 is one of the smallest Indian nations in the country. They consider themselves to be the keepers of the Grand Canyon, their "grandmother canyon."

The Havasu are also called "the people of the blue-green waters." This name comes from the spring-fed Havasu Creek that flows by Supai, their tribal center. Limestone in the river bed gives the creek its color.

Swimmers at Havasu Falls

Havasu Falls

Trail to Havasu

Havasupai Indians on trail

Supai is the only post office in the United States still served by a mule train! What a neat way to get mail!

Havasu Creek travels over four waterfalls on its way to join the Colorado River. Its most popular, the 100-foot Havasu Falls, is actually 2 falls. They end in a pool that's safe for swimming. The 190-foot Mooney Falls is the highest. Many people visit the area to photograph the waterfalls and swim in the pools. Because there are no roads, you can only get to the canyon by boat, packhorse, or on foot.

Wildlife

Last night a mule deer wandered into our campground. This animal is only four feet tall and has enormous ears (like a mule). It can leap up to 24 feet in a single bound, and it always lands with all 4 feet together!

Ringtail cats (cacomistles) prefer small rodents, large insects, and berries to camp food. The ranger said that some animals in the park can be dangerous, like mountain lions and bobcats. (He also eased our fears by telling us that they usually avoid people.)

Mountain lion

Bighorn sheep

Coyote

Chuckwalla

There are some strange creatures in the canyon, like the chuckwalla. This foot-long lizard's favorite foods are prickly pear cactus and creosote bush. To escape coyotes and other predators, it wedges itself into cracks in the canyon rock and puffs up with air. The Paiute Indians actually used to eat these lizards! The Grand Canyon rattlesnake is also unusual—it has pink skin! Its color helps it blend into the landscape, so it can surprise its prey.

The Kaibab squirrel has an interesting history. It lives in a 350-square-mile area on the North Rim. It's black with a white tail and tufts of fur on its ears. It is related to the Abert squirrel, which lives only on the South Rim, and is dark reddish-brown with a white belly. Long ago, the squirrels were the same species. But when the canyon formed, they were stranded on different sides of the chasm and developed into two different species.

Trees and Plants

Many of the plants found in the park were used by early Native Americans for food and medicine. One example is the cactus. Cacti flower in spring and bear brightly colored fruit in late summer. The Native Americans used cactus fruit to make sweet syrup, jams, and candy.

The yucca plant also grows in the inner canyon. Its "daggers" provided thread for making sandals and baskets. Other plants common in the hotter, drier part of the park are creosote bush, snakeweed, mesquite, and agave (century plant). Scientists once believed that agave blossomed only when it was 100 years old. Actually, the fact is that it only blooms once, then dies. Agave produces aloe, a gel used to heal cuts and scrapes.

Cactus blooms in spring

Grand Canyon vegetation

Agave plant

We saw lots of Utah junipers and pinyon pines along the South Rim. The Native Americans used juniper berries to make medicine. They roasted the pinyon pine seeds, called pine nuts, then ground them into flour for bread. Gambel oaks, aspen, Douglas fir trees, and ponderosa pines grow on the North Rim, which is 1,000 feet higher and much cooler than the South Rim. (The bark of the ponderosa pine smells like vanilla!) Wildflowers like Indian paintbrush, sunflowers, and rabbitbrush grow along the top of the canyon.

Phantom Ranch

We woke up early this morning to watch mule riders get ready for a trip to Phantom Ranch. It will take them all day to reach the ranch on the banks of Bright Angel Creek. On the way, they will pass many interesting buttes, temples, and other rock formations.

They will travel more than 9 miles on their way down into the canyon. Luckily, the mules are surefooted. They will cross a narrow suspension bridge 65 feet above the Colorado River. It was built in 1928. Mules were used to carry many of the supplies needed to build the bridge.

Phantom Ranch

Rock formation

Temples of the Grand Canyon

The mule handlers told us that they will stop at the Indian Gardens on the Tonto Platform. Because there is water nearby, the Native Americans grew corn, squash, melons, and beans here until the early 1900s.

Late this afternoon they will arrive at Phantom Ranch. It has a dining hall, cabins, and dormitories for overnight guests. It was designed by a female architect, Mary Elizabeth Jane Colter, and built in 1922. She also designed many other park buildings, including the Desert View Watchtower.

Bright Angel Creek

Bright Angel Creek is one of the best-known features of the Grand Canyon. It was named by Major Powell. The North Kaibab Trail follows this creek for about 14 miles. It is the only trail that goes from rim to rim.

The trail starts on the South Rim and crosses the Colorado River by bridge. It goes to Phantom Ranch, then follows Bright Angel Creek. It ends near Bright Angel Point on the North Rim. The trail is more than 20 miles long.

The Bright Angel Trail

Hikers on Bright Angel Trail

Bright Angel was also the name of a wild burro that lived in the canyon from about 1892 to 1922. He was named after the creek. His nickname was Brighty. He let children ride on his back. He also carried water from a spring below the rim up to the North Rim. He was very popular with visitors. Even President Theodore Roosevelt wanted to meet him!

Burros are not native to the canyon. They were brought to the area by prospectors. When the mines closed, they were released into the wild.

North Rim, Bright Angel Point

Today we drove to the North Rim. It's 215 miles (about 5 hours) by road from the South Rim. This rim is about 8,000 feet above sea level. In summer, temperatures are 5 to 10 degrees colder than the South Rim. In winter, the average yearly snowfall is more than 140 inches—almost 12 feet of snow!

Cheyava Falls, the park's highest waterfall, is located near the North Rim. In spring, when the snow melts, water rushes over the falls. The rest of the year it dries up like many waterfalls in the park. Point Imperial, which is also located on this rim, is the highest point on the rim. It is 8,803 feet above sea level.

Flower of the Sacred Datura

North Rim

Angel's Window

North Rim from Encantadora Point

If you stand on Bright Angel Point and listen carefully, you can hear thunder. The noise is really the sound of Roaring Springs, which is about 3,100 feet below the rim. This is the only source of water for both rims. From here I could see Bright Angel Canyon. It's a very long way down! The hikers with their backpacks looked like ants!

Later we'll spend our last few hours at Cape Royal and take the nature trail to Angel's Window. It's a huge natural arch of limestone. If you look through the opening, you can see the Colorado River far below. Nearby, on the Cliff Springs Trail, you can visit the ruins of a granary used by the Anasazi. The view from Encantadora Point is also really awesome.

Glossary

Civilization an advanced stage of human organization, culture, or technology.

Erosion the gradual wearing away by water or wind.

Fossil the remains of a plant or animal from millions of years ago that are preserved in a rock.

Prospector an explorer searching for something, especially gold or silver.

Ruins the remains of something that has collapsed or been destroyed.

Sediment rock, sand, or dirt that has settled on the bottom of a river or stream.

Spire a structure that comes to a point on top.

Survey to measure an area in order to make a plan or map.

Prehistoric before written history.

Pueblo southwestern Native American village consisting of terraced structures and housing a number of families.

For More Information

Books

Anderson, Peter. *A Grand Canyon Journey* (First Books). Danbury, CT: Franklin Watts, Inc., 1997.

Bruns, Roger A. *John Wesley Powell: Explorer of the Grand Canyon* (Historical American Biographies). Springfield, NJ: Enslow Publishing, Inc., 1997.

Rawlins, Carol. *The Grand Canyon* (Wonders of the World). Chatham, NJ: Raintree/Steck Vaughn, 1994.

Video

Grand Canyon (Reader's Digest), 1992.

Web Site

The Grand Canyon

This National Park Service web site provides much information about the park—www.nps.gov/grca

Index